Copyright © 2019 Noah Ballard.

All rights reserved. No part of this publication may be reproduced distributed, or transmitted in any form or by any means, including photocopying, recording, or other electronic or mechanical methods, without the prior written permission of the publisher, except in the case of brief quotations embodied in critical reviews and certain other noncommercial uses permitted by copyright law.

ISBN: 978-1-67909354-8

Library of Congress Registration Number: Txu 2-170-538

Any opinions expressed are only of the author and not of his employer, company, or brokerage.

TABLE OF CONTENTS

Introduction 02

Getting started 07

Leads and your sphere of infulence 16

Your website 24

Social media 29

Listing photographs 36

Video for business 42

Listing videos 47

Video capturing 49

Drone media 52

Drone imagery techniques 57

Photograph editing 60

Video editing 62

Your business 66

Conclusion 72

INTRODUCTION

Welcome! You've made it! To the introduction, I mean. Over the years—and through the countless hundreds, if not thousands, of books I've read—I've probably read one or two introductions, at most. I don't like waiting—I skip right to the juicy stuff! I always told myself, if I wrote a book, I would never write an introduction. Well, here I am, writing one. I think it's really important to quickly outline what this book is, what it isn't, and who in the heck is writing it—as well as what qualifies me to do so!

So, what is this book? This book is meant for any real estate agent (current or future) who wants to run their business and limit outsourcing by doing it themselves, to maximize the profits of their business. Outsourcing in real estate is HUGE. I remember when I got my license and all my information went public; to this day, I still get three to four phone calls a day from marketing companies or real estate photographers trying to get me to rain money on them. Outsourcing has a time and a place. In the book *The Millionaire Real Estate Agent* by Dave Jenks, Gary W. Keller, and Jay Papasan, they talk about using leverage to build up to having a million-dollar business. Outsourcing is leverage, as you pay someone else a portion of your profits to free up your time, so you can make money while they are making you money! That is a great concept—except in the beginning. We all have to start somewhere, and most people don't have the luxury of joining the real estate business marketplace with thousands of dollars waiting for them to direct to marketing plans and transaction coordinators. I was able to save an enormous amount of money by doing many things myself, like listing photographs, utilizing drone photography, using a free CRM program, doing my own marketing and advertising, and much more. The DIY mindset is especially helpful in the beginning of a new business because not only will every marketing company and their mother try to get you to hire them and rain cash on their heads, but you're new and inexperienced, and they know that. By starting out with my DIY method, you get time to learn the market and your business, and to separate good outsourcing from the bad. This book is also for that agent who may be leaving a large company for a smaller "mom and pop" company that doesn't have as many resources, like photographs, videographers, drone pilots, marketing managers, and more. You're all those things now, and the DIY mindset is what will keep the money flowing.

What *isn't* this book? It won't teach you how to model your business, but it will teach you which areas I found to save me an exponential amount of money, while doing it myself. This book isn't solely for a part-time agent, or a new full-time agent. Anyone can gain from the concepts I'm writing about. Whether you are new and have very little funds or are a seasoned agent and are looking for a few ideas to help tighten up your budget, you can find those building blocks here. This book definitely is not an end all or be all. All the concepts, ideas, and information I write about are pertinent to what I have done, in current times, as a real estate agent in San Antonio, Texas. Licensing changes over time; the way things are run logistically changes, too. For example, later in this book, I'll be writing about how I became a licensed SUAS (Small Unmanned Aircraft System, or drone for short) remote pilot—and by the time you read this, the FAA could have changed the terminology I refer to. It's always in the reader's best interest to complete their own due diligence. This book also isn't going to tell you to never outsource anything. One thing I always advocate to be outsourced is hiring your own CPA, at a minimum to just complete your taxes. Like many of you, I used software such as TurboTax or TaxACT, and that worked...while I was in college and made no money. Once I became self-employed, taxes become extremely tricky. Every year I file my taxes, I am sure, without a doubt, my CPA saved me more money than I am paying her.

So, who am I? What qualifies me to write about all these concepts? I'll let you in on a little secret: I'm not qualified. I know what you're thinking now: *Good thing Amazon has a great return policy!* In all seriousness, though, I'm not some hot-shot real estate agent that made it big, raking in millions overnight by just a blink of my eye. What I am, however, is an ordinary man that saw an opportunity, and I did make it big, in relation to myself and to my family's big picture. In just under three years as a real estate agent, I've made over $160,000…part time— and you can too! The first year, I made approximately $20,000. My second year, I doubled that to about $40,000. This year, I'm about to hit over $100,000! Did I mention, I sell real estate part time?

I became a police officer in 2013, and in 2014, my wife and I bought our first house. Through that process, I saw an opportunity in a hot seller's market in San Antonio. I saw the number of hours my agent put into my deal and I thought to myself, *Wow, she just made that*
much doing very little! Well, almost three years into real estate myself, I can tell you very much so that not every deal is like that; in fact, most are not. However, the transactions that are that quick and easy give me drive and momentum to continue forward in my business.

With that being said, my passion is to help people. If it wasn't one of my passions, I probably wouldn't be in two professions that help the people most—Law Enforcement and Real Estate. My hope for you and others like you is not to take this book as an end all, be all, but to read this book and my concepts and at least think, *I've never thought of that.* I love saving my clients money, and when I learned how much money is thrown away by new agents on marketing schemes or the next best thing, it saddened me. I recently watched an episode on ABC's *Shark Tank* where a business owner came in, gave a dynamite presentation, and when they talked numbers, it ended up that he was essentially broke and had an enormous amount of debt. Don't be that business owner. Take these concepts and use them, at least initially, to build your business without debt and take control of your business. After all, that is exactly what it is

—YOUR BUSINESS. This business isn't your broker's business, your spouse's business, or your pastor's business, it is yours. You are directly responsible for the amount you profit, and that is directly related to how hard you work, how excited, upbeat and determined you stay, and more. Real estate is a funny business; if you don't watch out, it can take over your life and your finances. I hope you take this book and do the opposite—take over real estate.

Noah Ballard / The DIY Real Estate Agent

GETTING STARTED

In the state of Texas, real estate agent licensing requirements include a large amount of education, as I'm sure most or all states require as well. You may be thinking about getting your license, about to register for licensing education, already in the middle of your education, or you already have your license. I'm confident that if you keep reading this chapter, all of you will get something out of it.

After I spoke to my future broker and decided real estate was something I wanted to do on the side, I began researching licensing requirements and education. What I found was a massive amount of options. At first, I found the traditional education and schooling, which ranged in cost from a few thousand to one too many thousands...after all was said and done. Then I found the speed classes, which seemed to be double the price but half the amount of class time. Lastly, I found online classes. Thanks to today's technology and the internet, the classes anyone needs for their license are on many online education marketplaces, and for a fraction of the cost of a classroom setting. The downside, as most people know, is you have to really have drive and self-motivation to complete an online course—I had both. The full online course was only a couple hundred dollars, and me being the frugal, driven, and self-motivated person I am, I decided that was the best option for me. I was still a relatively new police officer not making a whole lot, and we had just bought a house, so throw in a mortgage payment with that. I wanted to "penny pinch" every way I could, without sacrificing quality. I was just about to order the online course after a free trial when, one day, I was purchasing something on Groupon. Lo and behold, I saw an online real estate course that was deeply discounted. Right then and there, I paid under $200 for my real estate licensing courses. To this day, that story always comes up when talking to agents, especially new agents just completing their education. The conversation goes something like:

Them: "Yeah, I did my classes here, and oh, it was so expensive. Where did you do yours?"
Me: "I bought a Groupon online and did mine for under $200."
Them: "Are you serious?!" Jealousy everywhere.

Education Cost Comparison Chart

TYPE	COST	SCHEDULE
In - person	$800-$1,500	Non-Flexible
Online	$200-$800	Flexible Hours
Fast Track	$1,000-$3,000	Intensive

Now, in all honestly, only a certain kind of person can do online courses, and maybe you aren't one of those. The moral of the story is research, research, research. My father loves researching; every decision has to be researched, and everything checked and tried before a decision is made. He's the one who taught me to check the price per ounce on food at the grocery store; not many people I know do that. A little bit of research can save you a lot of money and heartache.

Of course, I knew one of the drawbacks of doing an online course was I didn't really have an instructor I could call up or go to their office and ask questions. So, I planned ahead. Once I completed my online coursework and registered to take my license exam(s), I purchased a few practice tests, and I did them again and again. I found a free app on my phone that you could use to view flash cards created by other people, and I found some for my state's license examination! For days, even weeks, I kept completing them over and over, until I made sure I was satisfied with my scores. Failure was not an option for me. I went and took the test—and passed! I remember that day and how excited I was, but I definitely didn't know how much my life would change for the better from simply selling real estate.

The courses you will take to obtain your license lay the legal groundwork for your business. Some people think real estate can be a get-rich-quick deal and they fly through the coursework, only to find out later they are a crumby agent that didn't retain any of the knowledge. When I had my first closing, it was relatively easy (not like most), and I couldn't believe the amount of money I made from selling this house versus the number of hours I had put in. I almost felt like I didn't deserve the commission, or like I was stealing it from hard-working individuals—oh, and that was after I steeply discounted the commission, since they were fellow law enforcement. I kept having that feeling, closing after closing, and what I finally came to realize and appreciate is that real estate agents don't necessarily get paid for the amount of time they put into a transaction; it's a combination of time, knowledge, and creativity. No one else is putting in the time and money to invest in their own human capital, and that's why your knowledge is worth so much more than ten dollars an hour. I say that to, first, make sure that if you have these thoughts starting out, you understand you're worth it. Second, it's important to realize that your education never stops. I was so glad when I graduated college and I announced to the world (internally) that I was done with schooling for the rest of my life! And then I started the police academy...which had high academic standards...and books. It's never over for us professionals—that's what makes us...professionals.

While I was in the middle of taking my licensing classes, I made it a point to work on some of the ideas in this book (like a website, social media, etc.). It was important to me because I was excited, but when the coursework got dull and my motivation dropped, I'd work on my social media pages to get them ready for the launch of my business. Doing that helped me to re-focus and get excited again about real estate, and I was able to power through that hump I had hit in my real estate coursework!

Okay, great, you have your real estate license...now what? From the minute you get your license, people will bombard you with "you need to buy this, hire this person, use this service, pay for a drip campaign, pay for a CRM (customer relationship management) platform," and more! All the options will make you pull your hair out (I'm bald, so I couldn't). I sat down and looked at everything analytically and decided on a few things. The first was that technology has taken ahold of the real estate market, and this became more evident as I continued in the business. Hands down, I needed a good laptop. Instead of going out and buying a brand-new MacBook Pro, I purchased a refurbished one from a dealer with lots of good reviews and a warranty, off of eBay. I paid probably half of what I would have if I had bought one new. My briefcase is my mobile office, and my computer is honestly the window to the DIY Real Estate Agent world—so I picked a good, sturdy one off of Amazon. A lot of the things I was able to do myself were through my computer, so make sure you pick a recent model that is fast and has LOTS of storage space! I won't get into the Apple vs. Microsoft debate here, because in all honesty, it's what works for you the best.

The next, most important piece of technology, and maybe even more important, was my phone. In a 2016 member-profile study by the National Association of REALTORS, they found that 94 percent of REALTORS used a smartphone with wireless email and internet capabilities, every day. I already had an Apple iPhone, but an old one. Initially, I made do, but when the emails and the calls start building up, you want to make sure you have a phone that is fast and has a large battery life. Tapping that screen with your fingers over and over again will drain that battery faster than you can say, "Apple is cooler than Android!" For the longest time, I played the power-cord catch-up game. I'd wake up with my phone at 100 percent, be down to 30 percent a few hours later, and charge in between when I needed my phone. It was actually pretty annoying, but because I was penny pinching, I didn't want to buy a new phone. Eventually, after a few closings, I upgraded to a much bigger phone with much better battery life. For those of you who don't necessarily want to put that much money into a mobile phone just for a bigger battery, Mophie makes a phone case called the Juice Pack that has a built-in extra phone battery! You might think your battery is enough, but if you hustle and business is good, even the biggest battery will seem worthless to you.

The next things I needed were a head shot and business cards to put my ugly mug on. I am lucky enough to be married to my photographer, so that was easy. Many of your first-time clients will be your family and friends—but as you get referrals, prospective clients being able to put a face to a name is huge in building that trust relationship. My wife snapped a few pictures of my beautiful bald head, and instead of going to a business card design company, I went to Vistaprint. I logged on, found the business card section, uploaded my picture, designed my own card, and *WAM* (queue *Batman* theme song)—I ordered and waited. Vistaprint, luckily, has a pretty easy design-your-own platform that allows you to upload any photos, brokerage logos, and more—then put it all together really any way you like to give you a unique business card. The business card really is a magical thing. I always muse because, back in the day, listings agents would ask the showing agent to leave his business card at the subject property he had shown his clients (this still happens sometimes). The listing agent would then collect those business cards that were left, put them into a rolodex or a file, and have a list of who showed the property. Today, most of the time, everything is tagged and filed electronically; however, some agents still ask you to leave a card so the seller knows you've been there.

Lastly, I wanted to buy a suit, and suits are expensive. Why did I want to buy a suit? So I could look good in a suit at showings or closings. I realized I didn't even have a client base yet, and I was about to spend money I didn't really need to! A suit is totally your choice, and some people dress to impress—that's your personal choice. I ended up deciding on a wonderful sport jacket from Kohl's, located in the clearance section, that I can wear with khaki's I already had and a button up shirt I already had. This allowed me to stay somewhat relaxed and professional at the same time, which is my personality.

Attire in real estate is an interesting subject, and honestly depends on your personality, as well as where you practice real estate. One school of thought is that the more professional you look, the more professional you are. This way of thinking has been around for years, and there's nothing wrong with it! But, just because someone is not wearing a suit does not mean they aren't professional, or don't care. In recent years, younger generations have embraced the idea that dressing to impress isn't always the way to go, because it's about knowledge and relationships. I fully embraced the idea that a polo shirt and jeans was all I ever needed to wear to showings and listing appointments, because I wanted my clients to feel like this was a relationship, and not just a business transaction. Relationships, if treated right, keep on giving, while business transactions eventually end. I also chose to wear a polo and jeans because I made it a point to get down and dirty while showing houses. Each time I show a house, I treat it like I'm there to buy it myself. I go up in the attic and look around, I go in crawl spaces, muddy back yards, and more. Try doing that in a suit and some dockers! I also sell land, which has just as many or more ways to get a suit dirty and torn. The other aspect of what you wear could be determined by what type of real estate you do, and where. In San Antonio, there's a good mix between business professional and business casual—but if you go further north, to Canyon Lake or Spring Branch (just outside of San Antonio), it's not uncommon to see a polo, jeans, and boots worn by the agents.

All in all, look around and make your own decision and do what makes you comfortable. The last thing you want is to be at a showing and have your clients read your body language as you being uncomfortable, when it's really the suit and not them! Sure, I like to get dressed up every once in a while for a closing or two—who wouldn't? But the more comfortable I am, the more comfortable my clients are.

Now, you're ready to hit the streets (electronic and physical) and sell real estate! You've got your license, your computer, your business cards, and either a tuxedo or a sweater...you decide. One quick note about a brokerage/company: The way a brokerage or company is handled can vary state to state, but I will say this—interview brokers. Meet them and find out if you will be a good fit, and vice versa. The three important things to factor in are: the commission splits that they offer, the training and education opportunities (as well as mentorship, broker availability, and support), and if it is somewhere you want to be. Don't just join a brokerage because you see their name everywhere; that doesn't mean they are the brokerage for you! Do your research. There are plenty of books written out there talking about how a good hire can make you money and a bad hire can lose you money—the same can be said with which brokerage you side with. Now, get out there and sell some houses!

Broker Interview Questions

1. How is the brokerage organized?
2. What types of advancement and education/training are available?
3. How are commission splits setup?
4. What costs are covered/not covered?
5. What is provided for my success?
6. How much broker support is available?

LEADS AND YOUR SPHERE OF INFLUENCE

Let's imagine you're walking around downtown with your best friend. This "you" character is in a completely different part of your life; you never became a real estate agent, and in fact, you think the whole profession is garbage, and you spend your time basket weaving, sometimes underwater...for money. You've decided it's time to sell your house and you are in need of a grade A agent to sell it! You and your best friend see a fancy billboard showcasing a realtor all dressed up, or maybe some marketing promise is listed on the billboard. You may mention something to your friend, such as, "I think I'll call her to sell my house." Your best friend may say something to you in the sense of the agent he used was amazing, or he used that agent you're wanting to call, and she was TERRIBLE! Are you going to give more weight to the billboard, or your best friend? Once you get into this career, you'll quickly hear the term "sphere of influence." Just like cash is king, referrals are king. Referrals generally provide a stronger connection between you and your lead/prospect because your former client, family member, or friend has laid the groundwork that's most important in every real estate transaction—trust. Without trust, there is no client, there is no transaction, there is no closing, and there is no commission. Trust is of big importance in obtaining clients, whether it be through a referral or direct marketing. If a lead is from a referral, the individual referring you is vouching for you— much like how you would take the advice of your best friend. If a lead is from direct marketing like a splash page, Facebook ad, or something more, to secure that lead into a client, you have to gain some trust.

> **Fiduciary Definition**
>
> "Involving trust, especially with regard to the relationship between a **trustee and a beneficiary."**
>
> by Oxford Dictionary

CLOSINGS

TRANSACTIONS

LISTINGS | **SHOWINGS**

REPRESENTATION

TRUST

There are a few things that are important while gaining the trust of prospective clients. Whether they are referrals or not, you normally have to prove yourself for an individual to trust you with their finances—after all, you are a fiduciary. That building of trust really comes down to your knowledge, experience, what you offer, and how you are set apart from all the other agents. There's a saying that real estate agents are like car salesman, or that they are a dime a dozen. Ninety-five percent of lead conversion in Real Estate is proving to the prospective client why you are NOT a dime a dozen, and why it's better for them to use you. Obviously, as a referral, the fact that someone they know and trust recommended you is a good building block, and often why real estate is a "referral-driven" business. But let's talk about after that initial referral, or any lead. Prospective clients want to make sure you know what you're doing. Buying or selling a house is stressful enough, and they want to make sure their agent won't add to the stress. Yes, you may get a client every now and then that has blind trust, but generally people want to know why they should use you, and what you can do for them. Market knowledge is huge, not only for your own business model but for showcasing it and proving to them that you simply—wait for it—know what you are doing! You'd be surprised how many real estate agents don't; they think this is a get-rich-quick scheme (spoiler: it's not) and quickly get their license but put no effort into actually learning how to use that license.

Your sphere of influence is actually one big sphere, made up of many, many little spheres, networks, and connections. It starts at your fingertips (by either dialing numbers or sending e-mails!) and extends, preferably into "infinity and beyond!" (As Buzz Lightyear said.) Imagine you tell your mother, "Hey, Mom! I'm a real estate agent now!" Your mother then tells two of her friends, who are wanting to sell their houses. Those two individuals are your first clients, and they each refer two of their friends because they liked how you represented them, and those two each refer two more clients! You're already up to 10 clients, all because your mother loves you. When you first start out, your sphere of influence is key. Unless you make the grave mistake of taking out a business loan, you'll have no money for fancy Facebook ads, billboards, radio ads, etc. And, honestly, even if you take out a business loan, the money still isn't yours. Your sphere of influence will open up all kinds of opportunities and you may be able to find a niche. My initial sphere of influence when I started out was my family and my current employer. My employer has a high number of Military Veterans and First Responders, which opened up doors for me to advertise Veteran and First Responder discount programs, which is now my niche. There are loads of other niches, from Military, to First Time Homebuyers, to Investors. My first two transactions were for my mom and dad, and one guy from work. I learned a lot in those first two transactions, and I am extremely grateful they both trusted a brand-new agent to get the job done—because while I was learning as much as I could, I still didn't know a lot. After some bumps, we closed both deals and I was hard charging! That first transaction you close feels amazing, and make sure everyone else knows about it too! Spread the word that you closed a real estate transaction like wildfire. Maybe don't walk up to the guy playing guitar downtown and let him know you closed a deal (or do it, maybe he's looking for an agent), but definitely post it everywhere on social media, or bring it up in a conversation about what you've been doing lately. You want everyone to know that you have experience and that your business is active; that helps gain trust.

Sphere of Influence

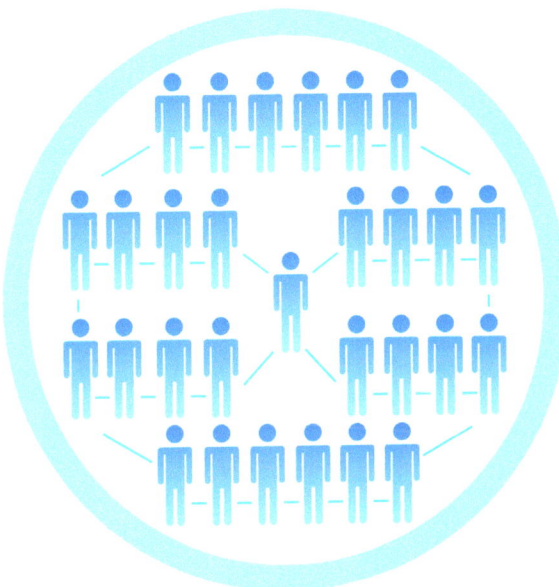

Niche Examples

1. First Responders
2. Veterans/Military
3. Farmers/Ranchers/Hunters
4. Investors
5. Luxury Clients
6. First Time Homebuyers
7. Vacation Properties

So, things are rolling along in your business and you're getting leads, turning them to prospects, then maybe clients, and then closed deals. Starting off, keeping track of two to three leads is easy enough—you're brand new, and you think about your leads from the time you wake up till you fall asleep, hoping and praying they'll turn into a client. At a certain point, it becomes too much for one person to handle, and you absolutely MUST have a system to track your leads. Starting off, I utilized a simple spreadsheet to keep track of my leads. I kept track of each lead's name, phone number, e-mail, client type (buyer, seller, renter, etc.), how they were referred (this is important; we'll talk about later), their wants/needs, and anything else I thought would be important to remember, like timeframe, date last contacted, and such. Each time I got a new lead, I spoke to them and put as much information into the spreadsheet as possible. What really helped was that my broker had put together an information sheet with all the pertinent questions to ask to gain a full understanding of your potential client's needs, so you can serve them best.

Earlier, I said keeping track of how leads are referred or found is important. Think of lead generation tracking like eating dessert—you don't necessarily have to do it, but your life will most definitely be better if you do! Why, you ask? Let us suppose that after two to three months, your spreadsheet has over sixty leads listed in it. When looking over it each night with a glass of wine, or a beer, or something alcoholic (seasoned agents will understand), you notice a consistency of fifteen entries that were referred through Facebook ads. You can then say, "Wow, 25 percent of my leads are coming from my Facebook ads! I must be doing something right! BAZAM!" And there you have it, the reason why tracking where your leads are generated from is as important as eating dessert.

If using a spreadsheet isn't sexy enough for you, since we're not in the 90s anymore, I present to you CRM (Customer Relationship

Management). The best CRM is the one you use. A spreadsheet is a very basic form of a CRM and doesn't have any automated functions. Now, I know what you're thinking: the theme of this book is maximizing profits by limiting outsourcing. Have no fear, because there are tons of free CRMs that you can use! The first one I ever used was called HubSpot. This CRM is a generic sales CRM and I found a YouTube video on how to customize it semi for real estate, and it worked GREAT! It came with a mobile app, so I was able to input leads on the fly, keep up to date with tasks, and so forth. I then moved on to RealOffice360, specifically built for agents. This CRM was sexy, had a lot of automated options, and more. Now, generally, there is a downside or drawback to the free version of the CRMs, such as you have a limit on how many leads/contacts you can have, or some automation options aren't active unless you subscribe. There are TONS of CRMs out there, and each and every company wants your business, but just starting out or with a small client base, the free versions should suffice! I have no shame in telling you that I reached a point where I had to upgrade my package and start paying RealOffice360 because I had so many leads, clients, and transactions I couldn't keep them in pretty much any free CRM there was, and I REALLY liked the options RealOffice360 gave. Do your research, Google it, Yahoo it, Ask Jeeves it, Bing it— do whatever you have to do, and I guarantee you won't be disappointed!

Why to use a CRM

1. Transaction organization
2. Lead management
3. Constant lead/past client contact
4. Task management

Example CRM's

FREE	PAID
HubSpot	Top Producer
RealOffice360	PropertyBase
FreshSales	LionsDesk
Insightly	SalesForce

YOUR WEBSITE

The first day you started your real estate classes, you probably thought about creative ways you were going to market yourself, your listings, or a house you would be showing a client. In real estate, marketing is ingrained in everything you do. If you post a happy birthday on social media —marketing. If you drop your business card in a free meal raffle box—marketing. If you smile at an acquaintance and strike up a conversation—marketing. Every breath is an opportunity to market. One of my broker's grandfather, Ernest Flores Jr., had a saying: "There's a certain amount of money out there to be made; someone gonna make it. It might as well be us." This is extremely true, and I wanted, took, and continue to take a large chunk of it.

First, we are going to talk about the online business card, your website. If I had a nickel for every company that tried to sell me their website that had all these crazy features, pictures, and super-spy gadgets, I could pay for all of them. If you don't have a good-looking, snazzy website when you're in real estate, you're wrong. I'm not just talking about your brokerage; I'm talking about an agent-specific website. Whether you eventually build your website's SEO (search engine optimization) up enough to generate leads is beyond the scope of this book; we're talking the bottom line of impressing the viewer. Remember how I said everything is about trust? Marketing is one of the bridges of trust, and your website is the entrance to that bridge. My wife and I were searching for churches online after we moved, and we would bring up twenty websites at a time. As shallow as it sounds, if the church didn't have a good-looking website, we nixed it without doing further research. In hindsight, as more mature adults, we realized looks equaling quality is not always the case—but this is the society we live in. It needs to be fast, snazzy, sexy, flashy, and relevant—or bust.

SEO Tips

1. Optimization for Mobile Devices
2. Start a blog
3. Use common keywords
4. Register with Google
5. Relevant content
6. Outside links
7. Register website on directories
8. SEO Audit

There are a few options for your website that can keep you from breaking the bank. The first is, you can read tutorials on the WordPress platform. WordPress is EXTREMELY easy to use. I went out and purchased some web hosting for approximately $2.99 a month and I paid yearly. You don't need a whole bunch of hosting unless your website has an enormous amount of traffic being driven to it. I installed WordPress through a super easy control panel (following the tutorials) and logged in. I went to the options panel, uploaded a free WordPress theme for real estate agents, and BAM—I had a website. Now, obviously, it took a few days to a week of customizing it with my pictures, content, and more—but it was there. For those of you that don't think you can go this route, or simply don't want to—do not fear. A second option is to Google the free WordPress themes for real estate agents and find one you like. Once you've downloaded that file, head on over to my favorite website, fiverr.com. On there, just search "WordPress," and I guarantee you that you'll be able to find a service that says they'll install any WordPress theme on your website for a few dollars. In either case, YouTube is your friend. Say it with me, "YouTube...is...my...friend." Some web hosting providers will set them up for you too!

Website Alternatives

1. Wix
2. Placester
3. Easy Agent Pro

You've got your website up and running…now what content do you put in it? My website is www.alamo-homes.com currently, and I'll give you a quick synopsis of the content I have there. I have a picture of me—people want a face to a name. They want to know what the man or woman who will be privy to their finances actually looks like! Next, I make sure to have the basics of what I offer/promise my clients. I have in there that I provide expert negotiations, drone imagery, social media advertisements, professional listing photographs, and more. Give them an idea of what they get when they use you; they'd like to know. I also have information about our First Responder discount program. If you don't have one, I still highly suggest maybe putting some information about a down payment assistance program, moving program, or some type of other "program" that would help pique people's interest. Testimonials, testimonials, testimonials. These are extremely important! You want someone browsing your website to see that you're a proven agent and that past clients had great experiences with you. This helps cultivate the trust that's forming between you and the prospective client—and you might not have even met them yet! Lastly, I have a blog in order to assist with my SEO and provide relevant content for the area, and I have my contact information so someone can actually contact me straight from my website.

Website Content

1. Profile/Headshot
2. Marketing Plan
3. Programs
4. Neighborhood Info
5. Testimonials
6. Blog
7. Property Search

Blog Ideas

1. Down Payment Programs
2. Neighborhood Spotlights
3. Featured Listings
4. Local Activities
5. Investment Ideas
6. Market Insights
7. School Spotlights
8. Local Business Spotlights

SOCIAL MEDIA

And now, a little bit about social media. Okay, a lot about social media! Platforms like Facebook, Instagram, SnapChat—heck, even the old Myspace—have revolutionized the real estate business. What once was normal—to bombard your sphere of influence with direct mail, phone calls, pop-by gifts, and more—has been supplemented, and some argue replaced, with a simple status update. These platforms have digitized your sphere of influence and made creating connections simpler, quicker, and cheaper than in the past. If you are not pushing your brand on social media, you're wrong. At the time of writing this, the two platforms that lead the charge are Facebook and Instagram.

First, let's talk about your personal page. You most likely already have a personal page and definitely need to read the terms of use regarding pushing your brand and business on it. Many agents use their personal page for all their real estate business branding, but they could be at risk of having their account deleted! The safest thing is to create a business page, and simply share everything you post on that page to your personal page. This helps with exposure/views/hits on all the content you post!

Setting up your business Facebook page and Instagram account needs to be a top priority on your list. In fact, when I was taking my licensing courses, I set it all up so the day I was official, I made everything public and everything got rolling! Telling your friends and family you are a newly licensed real estate agent is the first bit of advertising you should do. In the old days, that took whipping out your phone book and calling each one, and/or sending a letter or postcard to each one. While some agents still do this, you now can do essentially the same thing by posting a status like, "Proud to now call myself a licensed Real Estate agent! If you know anyone looking to buy or sell, contact me!" In all honesty, I actually hate the phrase "looking to buy or sell" because it sound too cliché; I usually say something more along the lines of, "If you know someone looking for an honest and experienced Realtor that will fight for them and treat them like family, contact me!" Disclaimer: I'm a licensed Realtor, so I can use that term in reference to myself!

> **REALTOR® Definition**
>
> "REALTOR® is a federally registered collective membership mark which identifies a real estate professional who is member of the NATIONAL ASSOCIATION OF REALTORS® and subscribes to its strict Code of Ethics."
> By The National Association of REALTORS®

There are many ways to setup your business pages. My methodology is to just do what I feel best aligns with me and my requirements. When you get into it, you may feel like a different style or layout better fits you and your personality. You can see my Facebook page at www.facebook.com/alamohomessa. Since the majority of my business is in San Antonio, I chose a vanity name, URL, and more to reflect "The Alamo." I use AlamoHomesSA for all my usernames, my social media URLs, and my website www.alamo-homes.com.

There are a few must-haves on your business page. First, let's upload that dashing headshot that you used for your business cards and make it your profile picture. Next, you'll want to fill in all your contact information, about information, and maybe a few extra photographs of yourself or some houses. You definitely want to make sure your social media pages are compliant with any state and national disclosures that are required on any place of business (digital, online, etc.). Lastly, and maybe one of the most important, is the reviews or testimonials section. This is extremely important, because you want a place on social media where clients, or even other agents who interact with you (rare occasions), can leave a positive review so potential clients can see that not only are you working hard and have experience, but the experiences of your clients have been positive! Good reviews help to reinforce the trust from a referral from your sphere of influence, and help encourage further trust from a prospect that didn't come from your sphere. Aside from these things, all social media platforms have the basics built in, like statuses, photo and video posting, analytics, etc.

Now, what do we do with our business social media? Do we post pictures of what we are eating today? Our kids? Random houses? Our listings? All of the above, and more. The best way to utilize your social media is content! People love content and education. If no one has told you yet, being a real estate agent prominently means you'll have to continually educate your clients, especially first-time home buyers or sellers. When prospects see the content you provide, they instantly have a connection. When you teach them something from content you provided on social media, those individuals subconsciously remember they learned that information from you. With that in mind, you want to make sure your content is relevant, and follows the 80/20 rule. The 80/20 rule, simply put, means 80 percent of the time, you post generic and personalized content, whereas 20 percent of the time, you post specific market or business-related content. The 80 percent encompasses a little bit of a lot—family photos or videos, personal photos or videos, videos of you out doing showings, what you're eating, something funny you saw, etc. The 20 percent encompasses very specific items, like infographics showing your market statistics, staging tips for new listings, down payment programs for First Responders, and more. The reason for this rule is, in the big picture, you want to keep your viewers engaged; if you rapid-fire all your content regarding statistics and tips, people will just skip over your posts. You want to tactically insert your engaging and informative content in between personal posts. People love seeing what's going on in everyone else's lives; it's kind of like an escape—and we're going to use that.

1. Market Insights
2. Down Payment Programs
3. Listing Videos
4. Educational

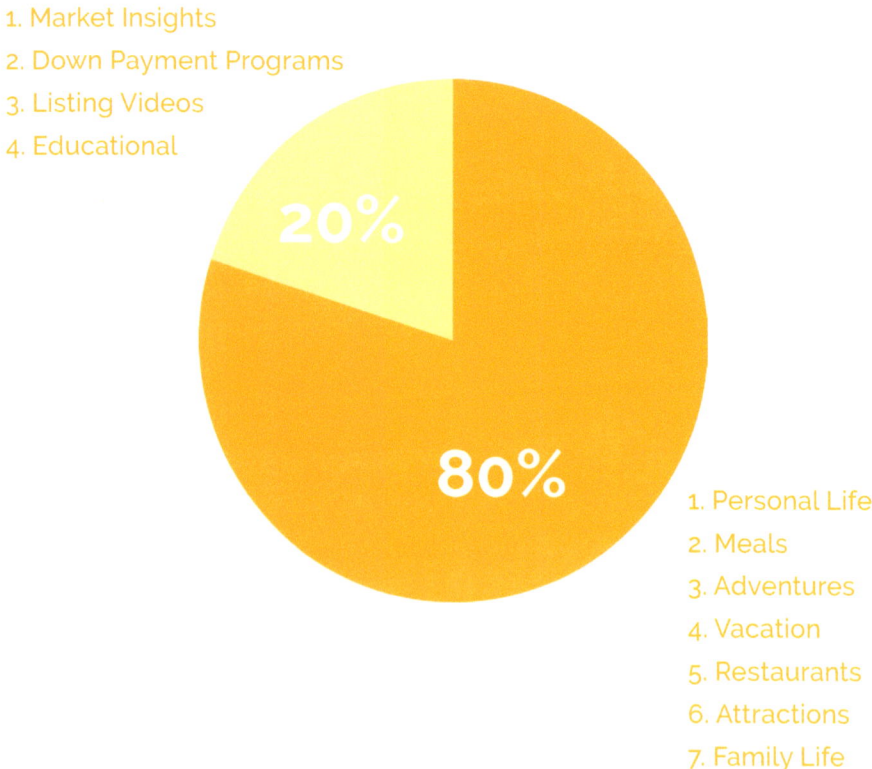

1. Personal Life
2. Meals
3. Adventures
4. Vacation
5. Restaurants
6. Attractions
7. Family Life

When I started out in Real Estate, I had plenty of time, so posting on social media every day wasn't an issue—and for some agents, it never is. A great concept I discovered when I started to get busy was scheduling my social media posts. Facebook lets you do it on the admin dashboard of your business page, and I also started using a web-based program called Hootsuite. Hootsuite integrates all your social media platforms into one dashboard, so you can schedule and post to all your platforms at once, instead of having to do it over and over again. I would take one day each month and sit down for about an hour; during this hour, I'd schedule all the automatic posts on my social media platforms, so I could set it and forget it! Occasionally, even if there's a scheduled post, I may think of something I want to post as well, but two posts in one day isn't breaking any rules.

If you have any social media at all, probably the first things that come to mind when you mix business and social media is social media ads. There's an enormous amount of information regarding social media advertisements, like what to post, target audiences, video, analytics, and more. My best advice is to get on Google and start researching. There's plenty of companies that will want you to pay them for them to run your own social media advertisements. While that could be beneficial, remember: we are on a budget! When I first started out, I simply "boosted" posts on Facebook and Instagram so more of my sphere/network would see what I was doing. An important task is, when you receive any "likes" on your posts or advertisements, you're able to invite that person to like your page—this helps build your social media sphere to reach even more people. Social media advertisements can get extremely fancy, complicated, and expensive—but a little research, whether online or in a book (maybe even a class), can help you maximize their usefulness. Not only do the advertisements help with your brand awareness and "touches" into your sphere of influence, they can also help market your listings, which is a big selling point to potential sellers! A word to the wise, however, is to try and not get frustrated with the advertisements—their algorithms change almost daily, it seems, and what might work extremely well one day might not the next. Social media advertising is a dynamic arena, and to be continually effective at it, you have to stay on top of it—all of it.

LISTING PHOTOGRAPHS

A husband and wife want to buy a house. They hop online and start browsing websites with home listings—what's the first thing that catches their eye? It might be the price, it might be the address…but, almost always, it's the picture(s). I've talked about setting yourself apart from other agents, and professional-grade photographs are the way to do it. I encourage you to actually get online right now and scroll through houses. Out of thirty houses, how many of those have awkward photographs that show just a wall, or a floor, or have terrible lighting? Listing photographs paint a picture for potential buyers that is extremely crucial. If the photograph is bad, the potential buyer's thought of the house is bad, and they may swipe right to the next house. When my wife and I bought our first house, we were checking online, and the photographs weren't the best—I remember telling my wife we should just go see it, just in case. We walked in, fell in love, and our next thought was that the pictures didn't do it justice. It sounds silly but providing your sellers with pictures that do the property justice can set you apart from other agents, and I'll give you the building blocks in this book!

You'll still have to do some of the legwork and decide how far you want to take your skillset of taking great listing photographs. YouTube is an EXTREMELY helpful resource. Between my wife and YouTube, I have learned a ton. The two most important things to remember when taking listing photographs are 1) light is your friend, and 2) the wide angle is usually the best angle. I started out using very old and basic cameras; they were all my wife's old cameras. The best one I found that was relatively cheap and could get the job done was the Canon 6D. I bought it on Amazon, refurbished, and it was pretty versatile. I also purchased it because I wanted a camera that I could use for video walkthroughs (discussed later in this book). Along with the camera, you'll need an SD card for storing your photographs (and videos); usually, 16 GB+ will work for your needs. You'll also need a decent lens for your camera—I chose a 20-50mm lens that was relatively inexpensive as well. The last two pieces are vital to your photography setup: a decent flash and a tripod. The tripod is so important, because it allows you to let your camera be at complete rest, getting the most crisp shot you can get, as well as allowing you to go to a very low shutter speed, which brightens up a darker picture (we'll get to that)! Armed with these tools, you can take some great photographs that will set not only your listing apart from the others, but yourself from other agents.

Photography Equipment

1. DSLR Camera
2. SD Card (16 GB Minimum)
3. Wide-angle Lens (20 MM)
4. Flash
5. Tripod

The first and possibly most important thing to do when preparing to take photographs (and video, as we'll talk about later) is to get the property ready. To save time, you'll want to ask your client to have as much of the following completed prior to your arrival. You'll want all the blinds up open, and all the lights on. When taking photographs and video of the property, you want as much light streaming into the property as possible. This is going to help your camera take a much higher-quality shot of the area, and make it easier for you. Plus, natural light always appeals to people! Next, you'll want all ceiling fans off. The reason for this is, if the ceiling fan is moving quickly, they'll appear blurry in the photographs. Lastly, you want your client to have everything as clean, depersonalized, and put away (or even staged) as possible. Surface area and space are the names of the game. Make sure your client puts items that may normally be stored in the open out of view, such as a soap dispenser, toilet bowl brush, or some bananas. The less they have on the counters and floors, the more open and spacious the pictures will appear.

Knowledge of staging comes from experience and learning. There are plenty of courses and articles around to give you a basic understanding, but make sure your client understands the why. The why is very important, because you're asking them to re-arrange their life, essentially, and giving them a reason sits better with them.

When taking photographs, you really have two options: You can leave your camera on "auto" mode and it will do most of the work for you in regard to settings. Auto isn't always the best because light, especially in houses, is dynamic and different for different sections of the room. However, "auto" is definitely the easiest. If you want it to be fast and efficient, taking the photographs and concentrating on the angles may be best for you, and then you can pay someone on Fiverr to edit them professionally—which I recommend, regardless of which mode you use. Just make sure the photographs you have taken are bright enough; no one wants to make a second trip to redo the photographs!

Shooting in manual mode is definitely a learned skill; I was lucky, because my wife taught me. Shooting photographs this way can be extremely difficult just starting out and is outside the scope of this book. My best advice is to study YouTube videos and online blogs that explain the basics of shooting in manual mode, especially geared toward real estate (after all, taking pictures of a three-year-old smashing his face in a cake and a granite counter top are two different things). However, here are some basics that have helped me form the foundation for great photographs. ISO can be considered artificial light—depending on your camera, the higher the number (more artificial light), the more grain the pictures can have. Know your camera and practice with it; you'll quickly be able to figure out how high is too high. Second is shutter speed —this controls how fast your shutter opens and closes. The lower your shutter speed, the more amount of light your lens lets in. The reason I told you earlier to have all the ceiling fans (and anything else moving) turned off is, when you're shooting at a low shutter speed, any movement will be blurred, since the camera isn't capturing the moment as fast as the movement is happening. Luckily, real estate isn't moving, so we're able to get our shutter speed low. Shooting real estate photography, shutter speed and ISO are invaluable tools. Because you're using a tripod, you can go down to a very slow/low shutter speed and, in turn, take in more natural light into your photographs. This allows you to use less ISO and, in turn, less grain in your photographs. I typically bring my shutter speed down to around 1/15 and my ISO around 200— but this can all change, depending on how bright or dark the room is. Exterior shots at 1/15 will be way too bright, so you'll have to make the shutter faster and probably bring the ISO down. Aperture controls essentially the size of the opening of the lens. This can cause (if a lower setting is used) a more "portrait" look, with the main object clear and the background blurry. We don't want that; we want everything clear and in focus for potential buyers! Luckily, when shooting real estate, you generally don't have to change this. I keep mine set between ten and fourteen; this keeps everything on line and generally focused the same.

If you aren't using a flash when taking interior shots of the house, you're wrong. Using a flash is extremely beneficial, not only because it helps eliminate some awkward shadows in corners, but in rooms that are extremely dark, it can assist your camera in taking great photographs, especially if your camera is of entry level. The most important thing to do is learn how your flash works and interacts with your camera—and learn the angles.

When introduced to a room or angle that is very tight/small and will be hard to get, vertical shots can be very helpful—especially for bathrooms! Typically, if I'm faced with a very small bathroom, I will lower my tripod and get closer to the floor to take a vertical shot. Be wary, though, because even though my MLS allows vertical shots and they show up in Realtor.com, I noticed that Zillow.com and Trulia.com did not include any of my vertical shots on their websites. Hopefully, this is an error or something they will remedy by the time this book reaches your hands.

When taking exterior shots, it is best to try to schedule when you arrive around the time of day and which way the house faces. See the related diagram. If the house faces East, the best time to take exterior photographs is any time before noon. This is because you want the sun rays hitting the front of the house and eliminating as many shadows as possible. Now, it will never be perfect, especially because of those pesky things called trees, but this diagram can be extremely beneficial for your photographs.

Exterior Shots and Lighting

House Faces	Time
North	10AM-2PM
South	Early AM/Late PM
East	Sunrise-12PM
West	12PM-Sunset

VIDEO FOR BUSINESS

If you ask any marketing guru what the way of the future is, he'll tell you the future is now, and that future is video. Whether live video, or just video—you want it, you need it, and you won't regret it. Over the last few years, video has taken over in preferred ways of communication—Skype, Facetime, Instagram, and Facebook all either are totally geared toward video or are shifting to/prioritizing video. Why? People love the genuine feel of video rather than an infographic, or a picture with some text. Video is cool, flashy, exciting—and you can get a ton of information broadcast in a short amount of time. I remember during my third year in real estate (still part time, remember), at our annual meeting, my broker called three of us up to the front (of about sixty agents). This broker went on to say that one thing all three of us standing up there had in common was that we had all made over $100,000 that year—and the second thing we all three had in common was that we had heavy video usage in our marketing

plans. He was trying to make a point to all his other agents that video works—and for them to do it. That was evident, because over the next few days, my feed was FILLED with videos of my fellow agents, whom I'd either never or rarely seen on social media.

There are so many avenues for you to use video in real estate, and they connect to many of the different aspects I've covered or will cover in this book. The first, and maybe the most obvious avenue, is video of yourself. Showcasing yourself and simply having a one-way video conversation can be educational, and even inspiring to people! When you do a "selfie" video, it gives people a chance to build that trust factor with you; they are able to read your body language, your personality, and see your communication skills. Self-confidence is huge in not only real estate, but sales in general—and video helps to showcase yours. The topics for videos can be endless, but here are a few to get you started: "Just got my license!"; "The different types of loans!"; "How much do you need for a down payment?"; "Down Payment Programs," "Come see my open house!"; What sets me apart from other agents?" and whatever else you can think of. Be creative! When I started getting heavily into video, I really wanted to bring education to the table. Whether you're a first-time homebuyer, or second-time seller, you always need education.

You may have a client that has sold three houses in his lifetime, but chances are, he still may not know or remember some, or even all, of the process and important factors. To help with this, I put together a little series called "Coffee and Keys of Real Estate." I realized that I was getting bombarded with the same questions from each client, and a lot of my time was taken up answering questions. Now, that isn't a bad thing, but I realized with video I could leverage recording my answers and placing my "conversation" on the cloud, so my clients or even potential clients could get the answers they might not even have known they were looking for. I put together videos of myself interviewing my broker, an inspector, an escrow officer, and a mortgage loan officer, and I uploaded all the videos and put the links in one fancy looking e-mail that I send out to all my leads and clients, titled "Education." I've gotten tons of views and great feedback, with people saying the videos were very helpful! What's great about it is, I am providing individuals value with something I did once, and because of that, I'm able to leverage my time not answering those questions over and over, to continue to work and prospect for more business.

Video Topics

1. Open House
2. Listing Showcase
3. Assistance Programs

Some agents take to the "vlog" route and post videos daily, or sometimes twice a day. They like to record their day-to-day life, maybe add in some "funnies," and people find it entertaining. It's a great way to keep yourself in the forefront of people's minds. I've even seen people add in episodes in their "vlog" where they go to different neighborhoods and showcase them, or iconic spots of town, new establishments, restaurants, historic areas, and more.

They say a picture is worth a thousand words—well, technically, a video shot at 24 frames per second is 24 pictures a second, so that's 24,000 words a second...right? Using video to show off your listings is a must-have for your marketing toolbox. If you talk to many agents, they'll tell you, "Oh, well, I only do video [or drone] for luxury listings, or listings with a lot of land." Remember when I talked about setting yourself apart? Lots of agents have to pay someone else to take video of their listings; you won't. One of my main marketing points when I meet with someone at a listing presentation is that I don't care if I'm selling your $10,000 piece of land, or $1,000,000 luxury villa—I treat all clients the same and provide the same services to each and every client. Not having to pay someone else puts you in a better position to maximize the opportunity and set yourself apart. It actually does make sense to only pay for video on luxury listings, because it's not worth it for you to pay $200 for video if you're only making $300. The beauty of it is, you're reading this book to learn how to do it for yourself, so all it will cost you is your time.

Lots of companies will try to get you to purchase their pre-made marketing videos, but I found I either didn't like that they weren't really customizable, or they were too expensive. I ended up purchasing a yearly subscription to AudioBlocks.com and VideoBlocks.com—two great and affordable websites that provide stock audio and video. I use the stock video to make my own marketing videos (we'll talk about video editors below), and I use the stock audio for both the marketing videos and video walkthroughs!

Noah Ballard / The DIY Real Estate Agent

LISTING VIDEOS

A video walkthrough can help tremendously because it gives buyers the chance to see the spatial conformity of the house and better imagine the layout. When you use video, the viewer almost feels like they are there, and this can already start giving them a connection to the home. Out-of-state buyers like Military, for instance, greatly benefit from video and virtual tours because they may only have a small timeframe when they can view houses—if they get a chance to at all. Some Military will buy a house site unseen! If any potential buyer has viewed the video walkthrough prior to a physical walkthrough, once they view the house, it's almost like a second showing, further reinforcing the connection they have to the house.

So, enough. I've talked up this video deal so much, you probably want me to shut up and get to how and what to do? Well, my friend, you're in luck—let's do it.

I started out with an old iPhone. For videos of yourself, your smartphone is really all you need in the beginning. If you decide to get more creative, like creating something like a real estate agent promotional video, you'll want something more professional. Luckily, the cameras on the iPhones continue to get better and better—the one I have now has two cameras in it that
overlap, and it gives GREAT clarity. I went out and bought myself the Zhiyun smartphone stabilizer. If you notice, on any semi-professional videos, they seem pretty stable and not really bouncy; that's because they use (shocker) stabilizers! I used the stabilizer for my selfie videos, which came out really nice. I used it, coupled with my phone, to film one of my first video walkthroughs. Looking back, the quality was terrible, but hey—at least it was stable and smooth! You'll have to determine if using your phone for a video walkthrough works for you. By the time this gets published, there will probably be four more smartphones that come out that have the next best thing since sliced BLTs—so there very well could be another phone that gets the job done, but right now, for walkthroughs, I wouldn't recommend a smartphone.

When I realized the smartphone wasn't enough for what I wanted to do, I upgraded and purchased a Canon 60D and a Zhiyun Crane stabilizer. I personally decided to go for the 60D because it was affordable, and I could use it for both listing photographs and video. Next comes the fun part—the actual video walkthroughs. Now, full disclosure, I couple my walkthroughs with drone video shots. I talk about drone imagery in my next chapter, so I won't reference it too much here. But do not despair! I will cover it all, I promise.

VIDEO CAPTURING

Let's talk about capturing the video. When shooting video of a property, the angle depends on the type and layout of the property. I deal mostly in residential real estate, so all my references and examples are geared toward that sector. As I talked about before, a wide-angle lens is most important, as you can capture more of the room with less panning of the video. There are two objectives when taking video, and the first is to show the layout and space of the property. The second is to showcase the selling points (granite, cabinets, fixtures, flooring, etc.). I could go on and on about each and every different angle, but the fact of the matter is, every property is a little bit different. One angle that works for this house, may not be the best for another. When you keep the rules of real estate angles in mind, you will naturally be able to see the best angles for video. Let's take a typical farmhouse, open concept, where you have a kitchen feeding into a living room, and a large island in between (see related diagram). Your first objective is to show the open concept of that area, so a potential buyer can see that while they are making breakfast, they can interact with the people in the living area. You may take a shot from a far corner of the room and slowly pan from left to right, showing the viewer the entirety of the room. Next, you want to show the eye candy in the room, so you'll possibly move up to the kitchen and do some close ups of just the kitchen, positioning yourself so the viewer can see a lot of the cabinets, or lots of counter-top surface area. I personally like to use a "topdown" angle, where I start at the top, usually looking at the light fixtures above the island, and then I pan down. This angle is great to show some great-looking fixtures, the beautiful countertops, and depending on how far or close you are, maybe a little bit of the flooring. Remember, the house will dictate what you do; if the house has marble countertops but the floor is carpet, you'll probably want to take as little footage of the flooring as possible (or just put your foot down and tell your client to replace the carpet in the kitchen for the sake of, well...everyone). Some rooms, you may only be able to get one angle, like in a small bedroom. There's really no reason to get a second angle of a bedroom, unless there's a unique selling point like a custom fireplace, or a wardrobe that really leads to Narnia...those kinds of things. I typically do not take photographs or video of laundry rooms, garages, closets, or half baths. Again, the situation could dictate differently, so use your best judgement—but most people aren't interested in those spaces, or they are just a bonus on top of the house. Some different "walking" clips can be beneficial to your video walkthrough, too, showing what it's like walking through different parts of the house.

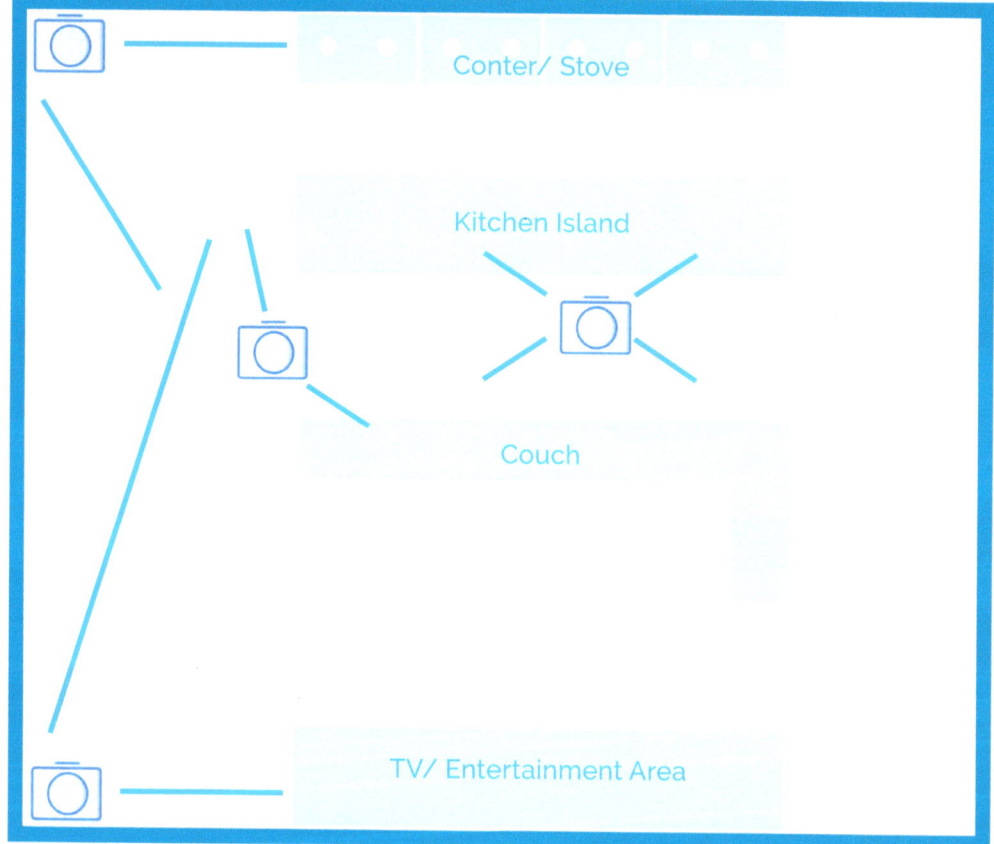

DRONE MEDIA

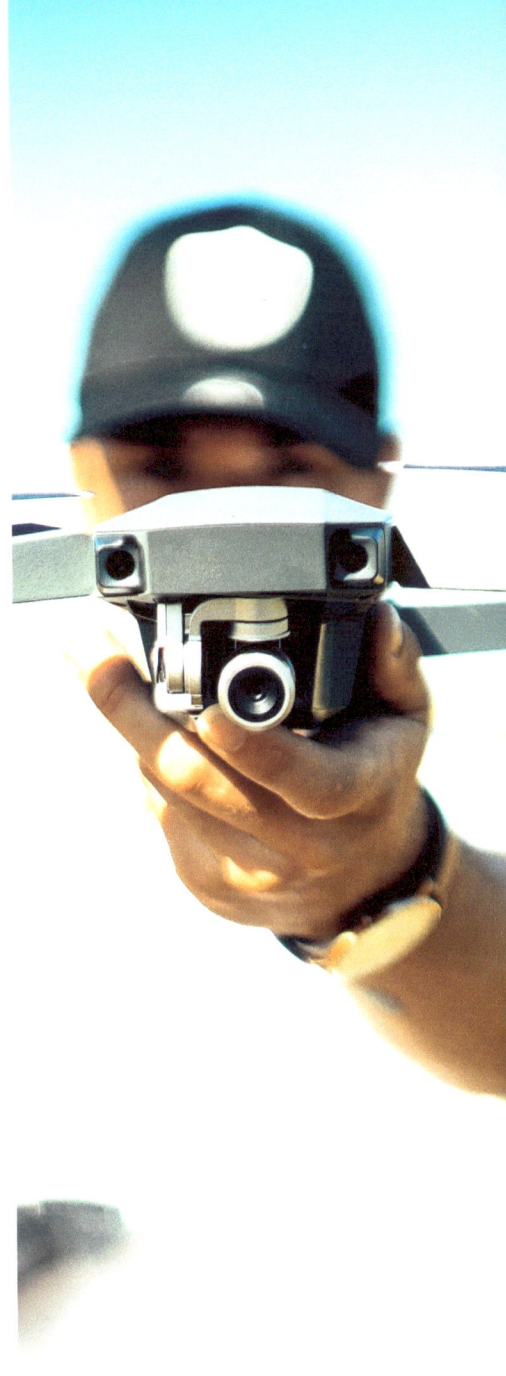

Drone usage and footage has exploded in recent years, especially in the real estate sector. Global investment firm Goldman Sachs reported that, "Between now and 2020, we forecast a $100 billion market opportunity for drones—helped by growing demand from the commercial and civil government sectors." - Goldman Sachs Research. Regulations have also been ramped up by the FAA, state, and local governments. Gone are the days of just willy-nilly going out to a property yourself and taking drone footage of your listing. Well, I mean, those days are still here, but with the proper licensure and insurance. I know once you read those two words, you started tuning out, but they actually aren't that hard to obtain. What bothers me is, I took the time to obtain the correct license from the FAA and insurance, but the majority of real estate agents blatantly ignore the regulations and don't carry insurance. This can cause EXTREME liability, not only for them but for their broker and their client (I am not an attorney, never want to be one, never will be one, so please verify liabilities with an actual attorney). Imagine you're setting up a listing, and their neighbor has a prize-winning cucumber growing in her backyard greenhouse. You decide to fly your drone for some pictures, but you don't have your license through the FAA and you aren't carrying insurance while flying. A bird comes out of nowhere and smacks your glorious drone, causing it to fall dramatically toward your client's backyard, and even though you see $1,000 sinking toward the ground, you are relieved it won't hit anyone or anything. Just before it gets below the trees, a gust of wind pushes the drone toward the neighbor's yard, and the drone crashes through the greenhouse—propellers still spinning, so it turns that cucumber into cucumber salad (minus the tomatoes). Not only could you be fined a large sum by the FAA, but that neighbor could decide to sue you, your broker, and your client— all over a cucumber. If you think I'm joking, look up instances like this one on the internet— they happen. Let's make sure you do it the right way, because the last thing we want is a salad of diced cucumbers in a greenhouse!

The FAA refers to drones as SUAS (Small Unmanned Aircraft System) and the "license" or "certificate" they issue is called a Part 107 certificate, or Remote Pilot certificate. The remote pilot certificate is, if one intends to fly drones, for commercial use— because there are rules. The certificate is not hard to obtain, but it will take a little bit. The test that the FAA provides is a test of basic pilot knowledge, as well as basic SUAS rules and more. Currently, the FAA only provides a few large publications for you to study prior to the test but doesn't really give any guidance. The best thing you can do is purchase a Part 107 prep course. I used remotepilot101 because they had good reviews, and the subscription was forever (you have to re-test every two years). The prep course was quick, informative, and helped me pass the test.

Part 107 Prep Courses

1. RemotePilot101.com
2. DroneLaunchAcademy.com
3. DronePilotGroundSchool.com
4. DroneAcademy.com

The second important part is insurance. There are lots of SUAS insurance companies, plans, and whatnot out there. The best that I found was called Verifly—it's a phone app. This company allows you to purchase drone insurance by the hour (usually $10.00) and gives you a very wide area that you can fly in. I usually get $1,000,000 in coverage. This is great because I'm not flying my SUAS every day, so I might pay $10.00 once a month, or every other month, whereas if you have a policy you pay monthly and you're paying $30 a month, you're paying for nothing.

So, let's assume you've done the right thing and obtained your Part 107 certificate and downloaded the Verifly app—you're legally ready to go, but what drone will get the job done? Luckily for us, we now live in an age where a new drone probably comes out every other month, and that's not stopping. The company DJI has a STRONG hold on the drone market, especially in many different sectors. DJI understands that consumers want reliability and quality, both in the drone and in the cameras mounted on the drone. Many people like the phantom series of drones from DJI; I opted to go with the DJI Mavic Pro. I wanted something that was entry level and not too expensive, but also had great stability and camera quality. We aren't shooting multimillion- dollar movies with these drones—at least, not yet. The Mavic Pro is foldable, which makes it extremely easy to transport and keep protected, and the camera shoots up to 4k. Fly time is between twenty-five and thirty minutes, which is more than enough to get the shots you need. Make sure whichever drone you purchase uses an SD card; you'll need this and an SD card reader in order to get the movie and photograph files on to your computer.

Top Drone Companies

1. DJI
2. Parrot
3. Yuneec

You're ready to rock and roll, and you've got your first listing you want to utilize drone imagery for. The great thing about some drones, like the DJI Mavic Pro that I use, is that the camera is very customizable. Just like when we talked about shooting in manual and auto mode for listing photographs, the same is true with some drones. There are plenty of tutorials on how to shoot in manual and auto mode with drones. Just know this: drone imagery is drone imagery; in this day and age, no matter what you do to the images, it's cool, it's hip, it's the bee's knees! That doesn't mean you shouldn't care about how they come out, but if you're a perfectionist, take a breath and realize this is a learning process. It's hard enough to shoot manual mode with a stationary camera on the ground, but when you're flying an object and on a limited battery source, it can be harder.

DRONE IMAGERY TECHNIQUES

When shooting drone imagery, there are tons of different angles and shots you can get of the property. The first and most obvious is of the exterior front. I personally like a take-off shot where I'm stationary in front of the house and then go up and over the front/roof of the house. This gives a great perspective of the main exterior of the house, the roofline, and the size (maybe even some into the backyard). There's also the normal pan shot, where you're higher up and you're drifting your drone to the right or left as you focus and keep the property centered. One great benefit of using a drone is to get better angles and shots of particularly interesting and marketable items of the property, like a pool, a barn, a circle driveway, a metal roof, and more! And don't forget still images! While it may be fun to get super high into the sky and get an overall shot—and there may even be a time for that, say, if you have a house with lots of land—most of the time for properties, you don't need to go too far off the ground. The terrain will also dictate the altitude you take the imagery at; hovering your drone at ten feet may not get as good of a shot, maybe because of tree branches, than if you took the imagery at thirty feet. You'll learn mostly by trial and error as you go along. When you're first starting out, take LOTS of photographs and videos of every angle; you'll be able to cull through them, and after you've done it a few times, you'll realize which angles and shots work for which houses and more.

After you've gathered all the photographs, video, drone footage, and more, you have to do something with it—or do you? Everything you do with your media and marketing really can go as far as you like it. I make sure to edit my listing photographs as well as all my video and drone media because I hold myself to a higher standard and want to provide my clients the best service possible (and I want to beat out the other agent trying to grab their business). I could literally write a whole book on how to edit, why to edit, what to edit with...I could probably write seven books. In fact, I think there are more than seven books for that very thing. I'm not going to say you have to edit each and every piece of media, because that is beyond the scope of this book, but I do want to give you pointers that are generic and can be used with any editing style or program you intend to have.

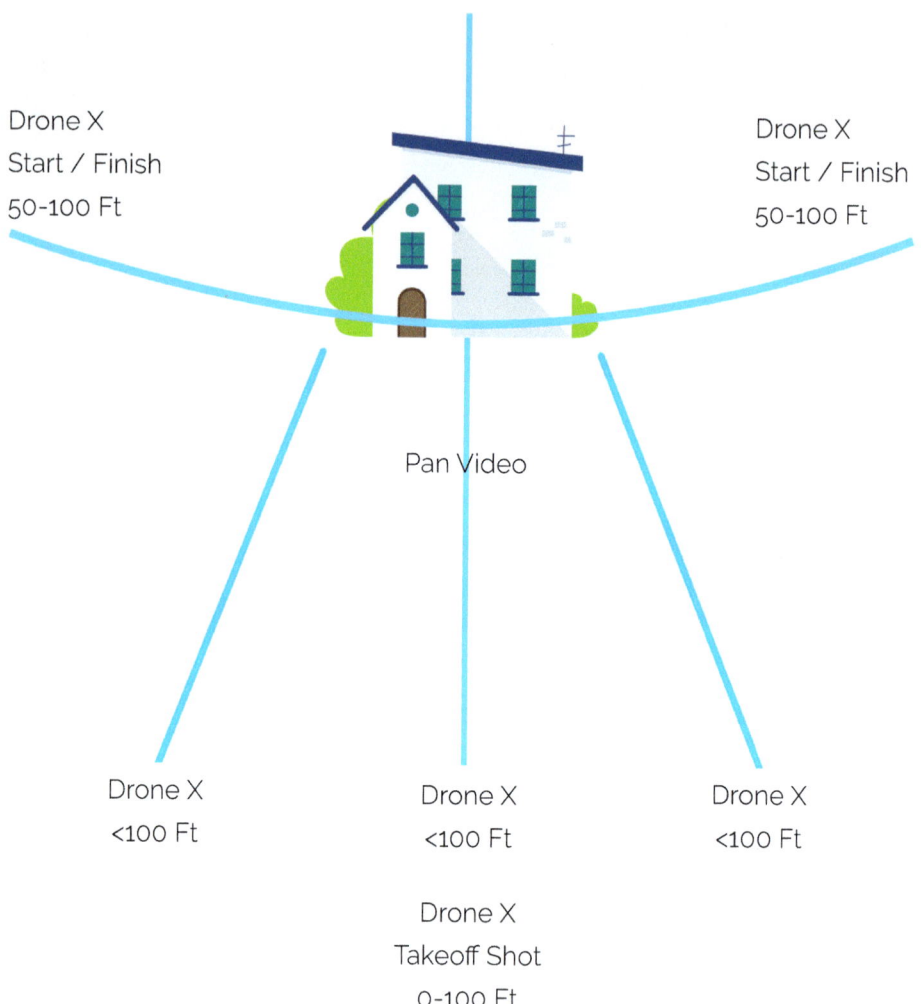

PHOTOGRAPH EDITING

Starting with listing photographs, the two most important things to edit are brightness and sharpness. Those two things really make a photograph stand out, especially if you're able to artificially increase the lighting of that picture. When you get more advanced, there are many, many other aspects you can edit, such as getting rid of haze, contrast, shadows, airbrushing, and more. Remember, we talked about sending your photographs off to a Fiverr individual to have them edited, as well—you can do that if you just want a blue sky or green grass (assuming the subject property doesn't have one or both of those). Making skies blue is sometimes out of my area of expertise, so I have a regular person from

Fiverr that does mine. A blue sky is extremely important. When I first started in real estate, I had multiple times where I put up a picture of a grey sky, then went back and re-took the photograph when the sky was blue. I had no showing activity with the grey sky picture, and as soon as I changed the picture to one with a blue sky, I had multiple offers. That's the crazy thing about real estate—one little thing can have such an impact!

Lastly, you'll want to make sure the resolution of the photographs (both drone and camera) match the best resolution that your MLS allows. My MLS allows 1920x1080 (1080p). When I upload the picture files into my editor, they are much larger, so I ensure to scale them down proportionately, so I don't have any issues when I upload them. That leads me to another thing—always, if possible, shoot in RAW. RAW is a file type that most cameras (drones included) can shoot images in. RAW files are much larger file types, but they contain a lot more information than a JPEG, they are easier to edit, and they have much better quality. If you don't shoot in RAW, you will be severely limited in what you can do to edit the photographs. Make sure you're only shooting RAW if you'll be using a photo editing program that supports editing RAW files.

VIDEO EDITING

There are really two parts to putting together a good real estate video: there's capturing the video and editing/publishing the video. Editing is probably the harder part to learn and accomplish, but also the coolest and most rewarding. You can take simple-looking video shots and turn them into cinematic experiences loaded with information and eye candy! There's lots of programs to choose from, but the two that stood out were Final Cut Pro X and Adobe Premiere Pro. Both are REALLY great, but I chose to go the Final Cut Pro route because I had a Mac, and I had already used the free movie editor they had and they had sort of the same layout and functionality. Learning to edit

video is no easy task, and you kind of need to really be interested in it. If you have no interest in editing videos, you should be able to find a freelancer that can on those marketplaces like Fiverr— but you won't have as much control over the final product. I recommend learning at least the basics of your editing software, even if you use a free version— something so you can cut, slice, move video clips, and add text overlays/pictures.

Video Editors

FREE	PAID
iMovie	Final Cut Pro X
HitFilm	Adobe Premiere
DaVinci Resolve	Corel
VideoPad	Hero

When editing videos, there's many different avenues and they depend on what type of video you are putting together. When putting together a property video, it's important to have something eye-catching about the property in the very beginning; this helps get the viewer's attention and increases the chance that he or she will watch more of it and gain more interest. Definitely make sure to include the property address, as well as your contact information. I usually put the address in the beginning and my contact information last—if they are interested enough in the property to contact me, they'll watch the whole video and get to my contact information. From there, you decide where you want the video clips. I take a pretty standard approach, as I start with exterior video (and drone video) shots, then I move to interior video, as if I've just walked into the house. There's really no good or bad way, I just try to stay away from showcasing all four bedrooms one after another, or all the bathrooms in a row. If you do something like that, you'll start to lose the attention of the viewer, so you want to continually spice it up every few seconds! Maybe something like exterior, living room, kitchen, study, master bedroom, master bath, 2nd bedroom, 2nd bath, 3rd bedroom, loft, 3rd bath, back yard, etc. I've seen it done before where some agents will take all the clips they have and make them into split-second clips that play really fast at the beginning for one second each—and then go back and play the full clip. This gives the viewer a very fast preview into the home and the video they are about to watch. From there, use your imagination. All you have to do is go on YouTube and search "real estate walkthrough," and I promise you will get a gamut of ideas for your videos. Some agents just pay for or have an app that puts music to the photographs and makes them look like they move. If that's for you, then so be it! Something is better than nothing, and I'd rather you be doing that than completely rejecting the idea of video.

EXTERIOR   ENTRY   KITCHEN/ LIVING   MASTER   SEC. BED ROOMS/ BATHS   CONTACT INFO

YOUR BUSINESS

The number one thing my broker taught me, something that I had literally never thought of when I first started, was that real estate was my business. Just because I had my license parked with a broker—and used his company trademarks, name, and philosophy—did not mean I didn't have control over my business. I learned, mostly by trial and error, a lot of business aspects during my first year in real estate, and I'm still learning. Hopefully, I can help you master these aspects of business faster than I did and lead you to be even more successful than you already are.

You are your own boss; you are an entrepreneur with your own real estate business. With that being said, one of the things I will never recommend you do yourself is taxes. Notice how the book is titled "how to LIMIT outsourcing," not "eradicate outsourcing." Taxes were a massive shock to me. I kind of had an idea that I would have to pay some taxes, especially since my broker would send me a 1099 every year, but the complexity of it all threw me for a loop.

My original thought was, I would just pay regular taxes on whatever was listed on my 1099. Unfortunately, it isn't that simple. Not only do I get taxed, but since social security and the other items aren't taken out, I get hit with a self-employment tax as well. Okay, great, lots of taxes—but how do I offset it? Deductions. Remember when I said this was a business? You'll have profits and losses, just like any other business. In any business, you need to spend money to make money, and real estate is no exception. If you close on a house and net $3,000 in commission, that's profit. If you spend $1,500 of that commission on Facebook ads, that's a loss. Most losses in real estate can be deducted, and a CPA is a GREAT person to have on your team and ask about deductions. I've included a related diagram, with some of the most commonly known deductions, but again, I am not a CPA and I encourage you to verify these with yours.

Top 8 Real Estate Tax Deductions

1. Mileage
2. Marketing/Advertising
3. Education Costs
4. Office Equipment/Services
5. Home Office Deduction
6. Brokerage/Association/MLS Fees
7. Software/Business Tools
8. Gifts

Taxes, self-employment taxes, deductions, schedules, profit and loss—it's all a lot to keep track of and calculate—and you just wanted to sell houses! I very strongly believe that hiring a CPA to, at a minimum, complete your taxes for you, pays for itself. I pay my CPA approximately $200 to file my taxes and I am confident I save that much, if not more, because of hiring her. Also, losing the stress of having to figure all that out is worth it! The best part is, you can deduct paying your CPA off of your taxes! Double win! But, seriously, if you still want to do your own taxes, research, research, research. I might even recommend so far as to go become a CPA (then you can have two businesses)! When I first started, I felt as if that $200 was down the drain and a total loss, but once I realized the value hiring a CPA brings, I'll never look back.

Record management is an important aspect of your business. In this day and age, everything is in the cloud. Every state probably has a different timeframe in which agents—or brokers—are required to keep documents relating to any real estate transactions. I personally keep the files in multiple places. I keep copies on my laptop, in my Google Drive (cloud) storage, and with my broker in his cloud storage. Not only will doing this help you stay compliant with your license requirements, but your clients will love you even more when they call you asking for a document they lost and you're able to give it to them quickly! I recently had a client call me two years later, asking for his elevation certificate because he was renewing his flood insurance. I sent him the certificate within ten minutes of him asking, and he called me to thank me a week later, stating his flood insurance went down by over half. I had nothing to do with getting him a better flood insurance rate, but subconsciously, he's going to associate that great deal with me, because I was still able to help. Next time he's with someone in his sphere of influence who needs a real estate agent, who do you think will be in the forefront of his mind? Me. It's also great to have the files in multiple different locations in case one goes down or gets corrupted. If you don't think it can happen to you, think again, and build in contingency plans.

And now for a word on staging and assistants. The statistics are clear, time and time again, that staging helps sell a home faster, and for more, rather than a completely empty (vacant) home. Unfortunately, staging can be costly, and it has to be determined who will bear the burden—the agent, or the seller? Will the company get paid at closing? Some agents take on the risk and pay for staging up front and write it off as an expense. I never had that type of working capital. What I was able to do was get the seller to leave some items in the house to use for staging instead of hiring a company. I learned the basics of staging from Pinterest and Google, and there we go—I had a "staged" house. Another great secondary option could be virtual staging: this is where a company will take your vacant photographs and add in furnishings for the listing photographs. This can be a good and a bad thing. This will help draw in potential buyers and help boost their creativity, but it can also let them down when they actually come to see it. However, as I've said time and time again, I think something is better than nothing.

It's very tempting to immediately hire an assistant, virtual assistant, or a transaction coordinator. I, myself, am at the point where I have just brought on an assistant—but if you're just starting out, or can't afford to pay one, you need to be able to handle it yourself. There is no right way to handle all the logistics of your business. The best system is the one you create and that works for you. Your CRM can be an extremely powerful tool in helping you stay organized (assuming it can help track transaction progress, reminders, and such), as can just your e-mail. You won't really know what system works for you till you jump in, but the best thing to do is to observe other agents and take bits and pieces of their systems and mold them into your own. See what's working and what's not, and evolve it all into your own system! All an assistant does is manage your business system so you don't have to, but you have to pay them.

After reading this book, I want you to continue to stay up with all the latest technology. The ways this business is constantly getting transformed by technology are astounding! It is up to you to constantly stay on top of it. I had an instructor in my GRI (Graduate of the REALTOR Institute) courses who had been in the business over thirty years, and he was (and still is) very successful. What I noticed the most about him was he continued to be on top of new technology, and he loved finding ways to do it himself and save money (kind of what this book is about)! Real estate is a dynamic business, and we must change with change. Using technology to go paperless is a great example! Back in "the old days," CRMs were done on notebook paper; today, they are all in the cloud (for most of us). Another example of going paperless is one that I just started using myself: using a tablet. I purchased the Samsung Galaxy Active Tab 2, and instead of printing out MLS datasheets to bring to showings, I load them on to the tablet in PDF format. During the showing, I'll open up a note-taking app and let my clients take the notepad around with them—they have the MLS datasheet right there, as well as a note app to keep their likes and dislikes written down. At the end of the night, when we leave the last house, I'll e-mail them the PDF of their likes and dislikes so they can talk about them on the car ride home. I've noticed, since I started doing that, that my clients make a decision faster, and I show significantly less houses per client. Technology is great!

CONCLUSION

I hope that some or all of this book has been helpful to you and your business. When I first started, I just wanted to sell houses. I had no idea the kinds of things that went into selling a house. Honestly, I had to learn to make it work, or (shocker) it wouldn't have worked. This book was designed so you can take all or part of it and make it work for you, your agents, and your company. Maybe you're a broker and you have a new agent that needs some help—this book can help. Maybe you're that new agent that needs some guidance—this book can help. Maybe you're a seasoned agent who has been used to outsourcing, but the market or business has slowed—this book can help. I truly believe every read, every educational session, and every interaction is a chance for us to learn something. Now, go out there and change the world!